how to get over

Acknowledgments

Gracious thanks to the editors of the following publications where versions of these poems first appeared:

90s Meg Ryan: "how to get over"; *African American Review*: "past life portrait *circa 1787, Negroes Burying Ground, Lower Manhattan*," "past life portrait *machete, circa 1791*," and "past life portrait *whip, circa 1793*"; *The BreakBeat Poets: New American Poetry in the Age of Hip-Hop*: "how to get over," "how to get over *for Kanye*," "how to get over *for my niggas*," and "how to get over *senior to freshman*"; *Cave Canem Anthology XIII: Poems 2010–2011*: "big bang theory"; *Cave Canem Anthology XIV: Poems 2012–2013*: "how to get over *for white boys in the hood*" and "why a negro would miss a bus over chicken"; *The Feminist Wire*: "l-o-v-c"; *It Was Written: Poetry Inspired by Hip-Hop*: "bop: Miss Cleo can't save you"; *Nepantla: A Journal Dedicated to Queer Poets of Color*: "the beautiful people"; *No, Dear*: "namesake" and "past life self-portrait"; *Poetry*: "how to get over *senior to freshman*"; *pluck!*: "past life portrait *circa 1849, after Harriet*" and "still life—color study" published as "july 12, 2013"; *SiDEKiCK*: "past life portrait *circa 1989, for Uncle Mel*"; *Sinister Wisdom*: "how to get over *Icarus as woman*" and "lucky number 7 (or indications that i'd be a lesbian)"; *T/OUR Magazine*: "past life portrait *as tomboy, age 10*" published as "tomboy"; *Union Station*: "ode to an African urn" and "why a negro would miss a bus over chicken"; *Verse/Chorus: A Call and Response Anthology*: "trouble man" and "past life portrait *Rodney King on Radio Raheem*" published as "Rodney King pens a eulogy for Radio Raheem"; and *Wilde Magazine*: "hands" and "how to get over *for Kardin Ulysse.*"

Every single word I write is under the auspices of my ancestors. All that I do is in honor of their omnipresence and divine guidance. I bow in praise to Lillie Mae and Otis Lee who I know have everything to do with this book being published.

This book, these poems, every single word, is the result of the love and care of a great many people including my Cave Canem fellows and instructors, especially the tremendous support and encouragement of Toi Derricotte, Cornelius Eady, and Alison Meyers. Special shout-out to Maya Washington, Ashaki Jackson, avery r. young, Mahogany Browne, Hafizah Geter, Nicole Sealey, Terrance Hayes, Chris

Abani, Nikky Finney, Natasha Trethewey, Jacqueline Jones LaMon, and Groups E and F from 2011–2013.

There are three people I cannot thank enough: Patricia Smith, Roger Bonair-Agard, and Tyehimba Jess. You took my lump of coal and helped me chip away at it until it resembled something shiny and precious. I am forever grateful.

To my family who inspires, loves, and supports me in all the ways they know how. Special thanks to my little big sister Tiffany Simone, who has always been my biggest cheerleader.

And Aunjanue, you've been such a kind and encouraging reader all these years.

All of y'all. Yes, you. And you, and you. Insert your name here _____. You, who came to readings, bought my CDs and chapbooks, followed my progress, and rooted for me from afar (and up close). I see you. I thank you.

To A. E. Stallings, for seeing and hearing my voice and to the AROHO Foundation. You made this book possible.

Finally, Tiffany Lina, how sweet it is to be loved by you. You lift me up. You hold me down.

sayWord.

Contents

love

die

how to get over

how to get over

Donyale Luna

For she is not really beautiful; but like her namesake,
the moon, she is different in every phase . . .

i.

skin: but not   skin—   *paper mache*   *eggshells*
sequins   *sheet music*   *painkillers*   any
thing   but skin—   *ostrich feathers*   *whipped*   *cream*
medical gauze   *strobelight*   *pearls*   *orchid petals*
rabbit's feet   any   thing   but skin—   *moonlight*
candle wax   *angeldust*   *toilet paper*   *tablecloths*
alabaster   *cotton balls*   *chimney smoke*   *popcorn*
anything   but   skin—   this skin:
translated into a language i no longer speak
pecans   *cinnamon*   *dirtfloor*   *treebark*   *alien*
dishwater   *heroin*   *brown*   is the word
i drown in   funeral of caramel limbs
but i am teeth too   a delicious white
& eyes tinted blue   & skin so skinny
you can almost see my bones   glowing

ii.

with my new tongue i learn new words for hair
ethereal   *gossamer*   *blonde*
the boys fawn over me—so different
than their nextdoor girls with whom i bond
over gin & pot   hot & sour soup at 3 a.m.
they never bore of me & my extraordinary
shade—the white boys wade in my river
this dirty brown runs   deep   but i weep

for a dredging   rid me of this rusty muck
black history & such   weight of so many firsts
to them   i am transcendent   a light beyond
skin   i am measurements   angles   hands
placed just so—a party of parts   not sums
the slums *colored* conjures   threatening
segregation   this celebration of myself

iii.

here is my offering:
a sloughing off   a chance to become
chameleon   coil of neon   a light beyond
Negro   colored   or some other dull
adjective   i offer instead   a full page spread
free advertising   history revising itself
something more ordinary than progress
promising equality   what i promise?
Paris   & a parade of flashbulbs   trampling
inferiority   a city of lights   brightening
you three shades   an enlightened gaze
a chance at reinvention   a naming ceremony
something feathery on the tongue
with the opacity of moonlight   audacity
of white—   where *moon* becomes *luna*

live

black, brown, and beige (a movement in three parts)

after Duke Ellington

Movement One: Black

work song

there is a graveyard in the belly
a hunger jutting crooked
like a tombstone.

a plantation in them lungs
dirt floors and hot air
a suffocated field
holla   a rebirth

a migration in the throat
a barefoot chant toward
some muscled music
fractured rock—
freedom roll

come Sunday

a river runs
through every holy town
its lulling rush like the breath
of Jesus. a salve for Monday
blues cause he the only white
who sees us. have mercy river—
forgiver of sins, we born
again   slaves
until Spirit
frees us

light

there is a tunnel as black
as singed bone
a congregation there
a chorus of winged mouths
a tunnel. a kaleidoscope
of echoes. a backbone.
a graveyard of grannies
searching for shadows
follow follow
black winged moths
into the tunnel of night—
a chorus of light slanted
like your church hat
your roof
the soles of your
shoes.

Movement Two: Brown

(West Indian) Influence

all this: African
that soft-shoe
that boogaloo
that cha-cha
samba
mambo
rumba
hustle
shing-a-ling
swing
slide electric
poplock
Lindy Hop
krump
twerk

alla that: African
that two-step
drunk with swagger
that limp—pimp walk
Harlem Shake Hollywood
shuffle
nigger
negro
nigra
nigga.

i
ain't
brown
i'm
Black.

Emancipation Celebration

how it feel?
weightless
a body burdened
colored—freed

what lightness this?
to walk as if winged
every step a sing-song
sway. a new breed

what Christmas this?
Juneteenth jubilee
a throat without chain
a book—no one to read

what reverie idles
this mind, these hands?
who will tend this land,
reap this cruel seed?

The Blues

what good free
hungry?
what good hands
empty?
what good mouth
quiet?
what good God
invisible?
what good skin
colored?
what good black
blue?

what good hands
hungry?
what good mouth
empty?
what good God
quiet?
what good skin
invisible?
what good black
free?

Movement Three: Beige

Sugar Hill Penthouse

this skin   a journey
a testament—a lynching
a litmus test see
how faces turn red,
acidic this skin
an acrid memory
tanging the tongue

how mundane this
skin   a shade
and a half past alright
a nighttime creeping
a bucket of fresh
cream—memory
curdling

this skin   a telling
a pointed finger—
evidence, a finger
print   a witness

come Sunday (resurrection remix)

this here   a church
your touch—
a tambourine
a quivering finger
possessed
our hands
pressed together
a prayer
blessed reunion
this skin
a bible page
a holyghost
in them legs
calves praising God
that run
in your stockings
the Devil
but every step
faith
every breath
religion
your glorious mouth
scripture.

past life portrait

machete, circa 1791

my widest mouth hungriest in morning break
fast   a staccato thwack clacking stalks of cane
sugar my smiling blade but teeth sharpening
themselves against the sweet dull thud of routine
rusty renegades of serrated jag thirst
yonder fields set ablaze in rebellion—smoke
blackening sky beckoning a thousand mouths
like me, but alas, i remain—   in boredom
i scalp dandelions, split plantains in two
whack my way through gorgeous ripe watermelon
but neither its flesh nor juice seduces me—
when the hands come to handle me clumsily
i flail toward lower ground threatening toes
dusty teeth lusting not for sound but blood

past life portrait

whip, circa 1793

elongated tongue—calfskin tanned taut
lifeless muscle becomes momentum
the moment the hand speaks   seeking
flesh   a succession of licks
a streak   dizzying crisscross
the back sings of blood
recoil and delicious sting
ringing out a warning across fields
no one feared the cow raped of her milk
slaughtered   hides weathered into leather
while the natives feasted on steak but at least
this second life, this freedom
all feeling   even at the hands of others—
a glory of sorts

why a negro would miss a bus over chicken

cause some shit you just can't get out your bones
we know no acts of niceness, chickens scatter,
smell the   sacrifices we offer in blood—
hands calloused and stained from the wringing

cause hunger is an eyeless hag with three mouths
open   a graveyard dirts our bellies
dinner is a funeral of singing   call us
bone collector   hear the clanking as we eat—

let the yardbird fall where it may

cause this feast of legs and thighs a luxury—
brown hands caked in flour seem like ritual
like black magic   like high priestess   divine
your life in the white dust on the kitchen floor

past life portrait

circa 1787, Negroes Burying Ground,
Lower Manhattan

The resurrectionists
smell unsettled ground—
a sun-wilted lily's
sweet reek

a newly nailed pine box
sticky with shellac
moldy funk of a borrowed
black suit, the perfumed

pomatum—the body
unearthed   undressed
a fresh wound   embalmed
a son, wilted lilies—

What lies inside
a nigger?

Are the lungs birdcages
filled with feathers?

Are the bones magic
wands of calcium
and rhythm?

Can the blood's iron
smith a hammerhead?

Is the throat
lined with gold?

ode to an African urn

for Trayvon and them
after Keats

what men or gods are these?
what mad pursuit?
what sin or odd odds are these?
what men or gods are these?
what unarmed boys down on bruised knees?
what mad blue suits?
what men or gods are these?
what mad pursuit?

what struggle to escape?
fair youth, beneath the trees, you cannot leave
what's suspect? brown skin? hooded drape?
what struggle to escape?
what estranged fruit? frayed rope 'round nape
unfair youth, beneath the leaves, you cannot be: leave.
what struggle to escape?
fair youth, beneath the trees, you cannot leave

who are these coming to the sacrifice?
whose bloodied hands shall stain the earth?
what eye for what eye shall suffice?
who are these coming to the sacrifice?
what's worth this brown skin? who shall pay what price?
or else why be born? why be bothered with birth?
who are these coming to the sacrifice?
whose bloodied hands shall stain the earth?

how to get over

screw off your mouth and sit there bottle-still. know what it like to feel fragile.
full of air, but no voice. whole body a lung, no choice but breathe. wait for sludge
or liquid or sand to fill you. do not budge unless toppled. almost shattered—the
ground fast forwarding toward you. the wobble upright. uprooted toward
lips. threatened in sips toward half-empty. empty: echo in the throat. choke
from the drunken grip 'round your narrowing neck. the passing of hands. the
fingerprints that dance along the rough song blown through you. the spit
sliding inside. consider how cracking could free you. how break and shatter
become you. how the glinting shards could draw blood—

past life portrait

as tomboy, age 10

i followed them—
the boys
who smelled like
rusted shopping carts
river water
piss

i would kiss them
these boys
who tasted like
grape Now & Laters
tap water
sweat

i wanted them
those boys
with hands fast like
pool hall hustlers
running water
threat

i wanted to be them
one of the boys
who walked like
youngblood
cool water
daddy

i followed them—
tomboy
with body like
cokebottle

bloody water
mama

followed them
pretty boys
with bodies like
empty houses
no running water:
wet

lucky number 7 (or indications that i'd be a lesbian)

when i was 7, i hoped rocks would whisper
the secret to being hard. fascinated by Keisha's skin
so soft, i seduced her into humping even though she
was five years my senior and my babysitter—click of the light
covers snatched away like a magic trick reveal
i could hear Keisha wail one floor up
through the radiator pipes—i was the victim.

at 7, i decided i should've been born
a boy, a he, a him. blamed my mama for her mistake.
prayed for a penis and practiced peeing standing up
until it came: aim, angle of lean, and straddle were crucial.
toilet seat up, knees clamping the cool rim i let go
of the golden flow feeling the warm wet trickle down my legs
darkening my dungarees a new shade of blue.

at 7, i was never afraid of putting things in my mouth:
i chewed my fingernails till they bled, chewed pencils
till the yellow paint flaked me a crusty mustache,
chewed pen caps into odd sculptures, chewed pens until
the inky cylinders leaked a Rorschach on my face
kids pointing as i ran to the bathroom
oooh a butterfly! no, a thundercloud . . .

i wore my iron-on Bruce Lee sweatshirt till his face cracked
and faded invisible. still, i felt invincible when i wore it
kicking lunch tables with my shins. karate-chopping pencils
in two. forever trying to impress the skirts with my awkward
brand of goof. punching my arm to make lumps
rise out of the bony sinew. at 7, i knew
how to make a girl cry.

how to get over

for Kardin Ulysse

your walk is a beautiful
tattletale. a big-mouthed
bitch with whispery rumor
on her breath snitching
on your every step.

        ugly it up with swag
        and butch till it becomes
        a butchered two-step,
        an abandoned stagger:
        lifeless line of straight.

your walk is a beautiful
bowl of sugar. brown
and crystalline. a slow
melt on the tongue.

        bitter that shit
        with dead cigarette butts.
        gather your spit till it
        dissolves all remnant of sweet.

your walk is a beautiful
threat. bomb. lit fuse strut.
a live wire spitting spark.

        what else is there to do
        but detonate? send flamboyant
        limbs flying   everywhichway.

your walk is a beautiful
battlefield. a loaded sashay
of sway and muscled thigh

        declare war. unload the artillery
        of switch. shrapnel their eyes
        with bitch and fierce. drop dead,

        gorgeous.

how to get over

senior to freshman

pick the big bitch:
the chick who look like
she chew screwdrivers
hunched at the lunch table copying homework
shredding syllables with a mouthful of metal

shush the rebel
in your throat, that ghost of punk funking
dark circles in the pits of your polo
resist the impulse to shittalk your way
through ranch dressing and lunchroom throng

bumrush: snatch
song from her ears, tangle of headphone
wires and tracks of mangled weave
nevermind uglying her face
with nails or an armful of bangles

she already a jigsaw puzzle
of scratch and scar, every exposed part
caked in Vaseline   every fold of fat
fortified with that free-free—French fries
chickenshit shaped like tenders   cheese sticks

she will slip-n-slide you
if you don't come correct
pick you up by your bookbag
till you feel fly, camera phone red eyes
winking your punkass almost famous

but that ain't your fame to claim
pitbull her ankles till she drop
till ketchup and corn splatter
scatter abstract like technique
from our 5th period art class

as she knuckles herself up
from chickenfeed, ain't no need to run
instead smile for the video:
that soul-clap in your chest
is your heart

how to get over

for my niggas

pull up your pants cripwalk and dance your ass off the corner coroners
got your chalk outline memorized bullets got they eyes on you du-rag
yourself an imagination   imagine a nation afraid of your brilliance
remember your grandma's resilience   her dreams—charred bits sludged
in chicken grease piece yourself back together get your dreams outta
pawn break dawn like babymama promises remix the lyrics breakdancing
on your tongue and play another slow jam slam dunk your way out the
projects consider yourself post-racial facial hair and funk don't make you
a man but it might make you a punk play dead when you body hits the
concrete like kerplunk hip-hop ain't your savior stop praising Lil Wayne
like Jesus   *nigga, please*: that fog ain't the weather it's the weed bleed on
the sidewalk and call it graffiti warn the youth with your reckless release
police know the sound of your stereo-type don't believe the hype: your
mans and them will snitch if pressed and your bitch hair is a weave and
Ralph Lauren is a pimp limp your ass back to school, nigga   triggers get
foolish in your presence remember that your essence is golden prison is
not your birthright nor sagging pants your birthmark know you are the
last dragon catch bullets with your teeth and glow—

how to get over
for Chaka

consider scream. remember urge
surging amber through marrow and bruised veins.
harness that gnawing yearn into timbre,
hide swollen ache behind lovely white teeth.

consider risk whiskeying your throat warm.
the truth and Rufus's musk perfuming
husks of lyrics you hide under wild wigs—
swig. remember wrong words to your songs
the ugly of your mouth, a moth
longing for light; flight through wild pitch.

refuse to lip-synch on *Soul Train*—
nevermind. do it badly. on purpose.
scratch the sunlight off your tongue like
lottery ticket. consider yourself
lucky. use the wicked gift of your voice
to fracture scream. sing me something: good.

shock and awe

for Tamar Kali

fuck what pretty wrote. she ripped that script
years ago. everything on her face, pierced.
her lips pout proud. eyes bulge bold, brown.
nostrils forever flared. and she ain't never
scared. head full of cotton caught in a bandana
like how Aunt Jemima and Tupac used to wear.

and although she guitar strapped playing that
rock shit, her ass got Africa tattooed
all over it. hood rats double back. she sing troubled
black girl anthems. her voice: part tantrum,
part opera, part street. where heart meets hard.
glass shards, flock of pigeons, in her throat.

and cats respect that. plus that ass is fat. plus
she can sing. 'cept her voice stings like eviction.
like fiction you assumed as truth. her face is proof
we sometimes superficial. choosing waterfall weaves
and golden skin over a voice that conjures
spirit and reminds us this music is ours.

how to get over

be born: black
as ants on a chicken bone black

as Nina Simone and Mahalia's moan black
as rock pile smile and resilience black

as resistance and rhythm and Sonny's blues black
as no shoes and dirt floors black

as whore and Hottentot foxtrot Lindy Hop
and Watusi pussy and pyramids black

as darkness under your eyelids black
between your legs black

as dregs of rum sugarcane summer
plums holyghost hum black

as bruised throat fieldholla wading in the shallow black
as ocean river stream creek running black

transparent translucent transatlantic slanted
shanties planted in red clay black

as funky chickens and chitlins and kinfolk sold away black
as auction block and slop and hip-hop and rock and roll

and chop shop and cop cars and parole and overseer
patrols and one drop rules and pools of blood black

as beige and good hair and sounding white and light-skindeded
and my grandmama is Cherokee, Iroquois, Choctaw black

as pit bulls and lockjaw and rage and hoodies black
eyes and black-eyed peas peasy heads and loose tracks black

as trees and noose and hounds let loose in the night black
as fist and fight Sojourner and Nat Turner and righteousness black

as fuck and not giving a fuck mud-stuck and quicksand
quick hand hustle thigh muscle and hurdle black

as cotton and tobacco and indigo black
as wind and bad weather and feather

and tar and snap beans in mason jars black
as nigga please and hallelujah black

asses and black strap molasses and turn your black
back on audiences black

as banjo and djembe and porch and stoop and spooks
sitting by the door black

as roaches in front of company and lawn jockeys
and latchkey kids and high bids and spades and shittalk black

as cakewalk and second line and black
magic and tap dance, lapdance and alla that ass black

as jazz and juke and juju and spirit
disguised as harmonica spit black

as cast-iron skillets and grits and watermelon seeds
flitting from lips black

as tambourines hitting cornbread hips black
batons splitting lips and Martin Luther King, Jr.

boulevards and downtown beatdowns black
sit-ins and come-ups and oops upside yo' heads

and we shall overcomes and get down on it black
get into it black let's get it on and get it

while the getting is good black
as white hoods and backwood revivals black

as survival and Trayvon and Tyrone and Josephus
and amen and Moses and Jesus and getting over

black—

lie

the answer

for inquiring minds

*Questions about his sexuality annoyed him; he
refused to comment on speculation that he was gay.*
—from Luther Vandross's obituary
printed in *The Guardian*, July 4, 2005

everything sparkles. even the dark glows
under my eyelids—secrets shame truth
in my name. spotlight licks my face new shades
as all proof fades from fierce to invisible
on stage i flash invincible. sequins
shimmying my black ass irrelevant
nothing left but bass line, voice, and dazzle
never mind reverend and amen corner
or employees sworn to secrecy. i
worshiped divas washed in gospel. swallowed
gossip like bible verses scorching throat—
praised Jesus and pretty black men swathed in silence.
my voice: a naked violence breaking into smile,
goddamn. did you really have to ask honeychile?

the beautiful people

sleep in make-up   wake up late   wait—
      for no one run down streets in stilettos
half-naked   verge of strip sip tea in the afternoon   curdle swoon
      into laughter   spoon   unfamiliar   spill
      red wine on white sheets

      and call it art

heart everyone who hearts them back   slack
      and get over—
    cover mediocrity with pretty
      wear it like a mask   suck at it
like a titty   ask and they shall receive   we've all given in   giddy
    weak
      they speak golden
        we beholden to every shiny syllable spilling raspy
from their   nasty mouths   eat fruit fed them by lovers leftover
      from night before   ignore
        phone calls
  fuck:
    in hallways—spandex screeching against paint   on stovetops—pilot
light scorching ass   so hot
      in the ass   they hardly notice
    quote   bliss from Buddha
      and other enlightened motherfuckers   sucker us
  with eyelashes   dimples   simple us
      stupid
        stupefy us
    with   one   glance—dance dirty against vodka
      bottles   ashtrays   triggers
  swagger us   into two months' rent   glint golden
    from glitter and angel dust   trust only

                      the glamorous
              glamour us and bear teeth   thief
our blood under strobelight   moonlight glows a parade
                in their honor
    throw   candy
            to the ugly
                  below   know
        we want nothing
                more than a taste of their sweet—

mercury retrograde

oh mercurial misfit moonwalking
planetary havoc and flux fucks up
town downtime downtown text messages be
come riddles electronic trickster slick
middle finger mastermind find question
marks sucking days' work clean from computer
screen phone calls unanswered gobbledygook
fluke hocus pocus blank screen focus flux
flower garden on my tongue mouthful
of thorns   barbwire   cow manure   shovel
balk and talk pigeon shit stalk status sulk
bullshit bulkrate cut rate cut throat milk crate
flood gate madness assbackwardness awkward:
no wonder why she won't return my calls.

namesake

sometimes they fuck up—fit you with a name two sizes too small & it
scrapes your shins & chafes your spirit down to sawdust & sometimes
the name too old for you—already rust in the mouth of a newborn torn
from some grandmama's past   her fast legacy simmering in the ground
& sometimes the name don't sound right in your bones   gathers in the
joints & aches before the rain come   vibrates your spine toward curve
& sometimes the name you don't deserve—too grand for all your regular-
ness it blots you invisible & sometimes the name is perfect   but   of
course they fuck it up—emphasize the wrong syllables   say it too slow
or without enough energy to make it glow & sometimes they fuck it outta
you—graffiti it with brutal memory   & one day you wake knowing it
must change

past life portrait

circa 1940, Lorain, Ohio

the doll
is one-eyed
the one eye is blue
like an abandoned ocean
in a Technicolor movie

the doll, a Cyclops
the eye all-seeing
never closes
bats or blinks
only thinks miraculous

oh the trouble it has seen:
the grubby brown hand
grabbing
the raped socket—a ghost
a bloodless plastic gutter

the hand's magic trick
the force, Pecola's
face—its elusive blue
eye a wobbling ego
an identity crisis—averted

the doll's eye, a brain—
an abandoned collage
of drying images blurring
the eye's easy release praying
girl won't think twice

how to get over
for colored girls

drain your skin of its color
till it tints toward beige

bury your rage in the back yard
along with your weave   leave it

for the scarecrows
when the hair grows   shake the naps

on ya head long and loose
till they dangle 'longside your neck

as familiar as a noose   use paper bags
to torture anything browner

than you   bitter their sweet with bruise
get used to pretty

pretty   pretty   pretty   shitty your 'tude
with its golden veneer

sneer at the dark ones
they embarrass you with smeared faces

remind everyone you are mixed race—
marry a white boy named Ethan

please him with the fat ass
inherited from the nigger you never knew

forget the funk of failure and its wailing past:
pass   pass—

how to get over

for white boys in the hood

quick—
get hip to this logic:
everythang we do
magic

slick—
da fuck you want?
ain't shit organic
but our spit

flick—
ghetto cinematic
dark documentary
put ya camera away

thick—
as thieves nigger,
you ain't a nigga
stop trying

chick—
the most beautifullest
brown you ever laid down
with   she try'na come up

sick—
wit it   but what we
got you can't catch
stop body-snatching

trick—
black folk smell

they rent getting high
you, don't say bye leave

quick—
grab ya camera
flicker black versus boys in blue
everythang they do: tragic.

how to get over

for Kanye

go spastic when the white chick win sequester yourself for the semester flunk
the fuck out   high bid studio time   study ya rhyme   rape crates of classics
for a hook   loop-da-loop   get stoopid   on the track
Louis Vuitton your look   crooked your grin when the blogs
        you read   read you
                                        let   niggas   know
how much they need   you   indeed you brilliant
be patient   till they get a clue   in the meantime   let it do what it
due: kick a mean rhyme   lace a bassline   waste time
on fashion   blueprint   niggerness   for white chicks
who have considered   bigger dicks when black myth   wasn't enough
bootleg Black & call it *Otis*   trademark swag.   call it: *Niggas
in Paris* call it   i'm so fly—i'm jetlagged   copyright your elbow ash
stash black egos in Marc Jacobs bags   & sell it back to us for undisclosed
                                        amounts of cash
and you know this   put white folk on notice
call 'em racist   to their faces   ball so hard   motherfuckers
try to find you   remind us: *we aint even 'posed to be here*
mercy us a theme song to dream on   fuck brilliance—call it capitalism *swerve*
        get what you deserve: a Kardashian & a mouthful of flashy
                        swerve—

56

wilding

for Antron McCray, Kevin Richardson,
Raymond Santana, Kharey Wise, and
Yusef Salaam

n.

1. A plant that grows wild or has escaped from
cultivation, especially a wild apple tree or its fruit.

> South: wild niggers grow
> on trees. limbs snapped, weighted with
> unfamiliar fruit

2. A wild animal.

> they wield rope. hoses.
> whips. rifles. hounds. cigarettes.
> machetes. spit. teeth.

3. *Slang* The act or practice of going about in a
group threatening, robbing, or attacking others.

> a woman: white—runs
> becomes broken silhouette
> brown boys go to jail

adj.

1. Growing wild; not cultivated.

> she naked as a weed.
> they feed on fodder: boredom
> heat   testosterone—

2. Undomesticated.

everywhere we grow:
wild—this land unforgiving
soil of bone and blood

past life self-portrait

circa 1979, Atlanta

this basement :: damp cement

little girl & her curiosity come tumbling down steps into a familiar darkness. a
family of hands fumbling. the soft sound of bible pages. a prayer? a mumbling. a
hardening. a dumb clumsy thing this voice—a cobwebbed water heater boiling
(secret)ion into spit.

this place meant :: damn semen

penis grows amid the bush. a wet whisper: *come here.* a zip. unzip. a fuzzy taste
tickling. a dingaling. dangling. a push. a strangling. a dank stank gathering. a
mouth. a festival of dirt. a tongue. a festering—blur & blurt. stutter & spurt.
what can bloom but lies?

displacement :: damned, see men

i do not belong here: this place: basement. cement. semen. see men. demon.
damn. damned. sham. shame. shamed. damn shame. this place. dislodged.
misplaced. dislocated. replaced. displaced—is that my mouth

balled tight & honest as a fist?

past life portrait

circa 1948, Peoria, Illinois

panties be cockblocking
& blocked cocks don't pay the light bill
so we don't wear 'em
just one less garment to wash
drip-drying from the shower rod

Bible bitches forever tapping my door
yapping 'bout the power of God
but niggas round here praise pussy
and a hot plate a food so the lord
gon' have to wait till i'm good & ready

plus prayer ain't never paid my rent
last time i went to church steady
every pew whispered hussy
hushed judgments knocking my hat askew—
i can make better use of sequins

gotta bathtub full of bootleg
every lover get a ladle of moonshine
noontime Bubbas pay double for effort
yet, on cloudy days i gargle egg yolk
pretend the sun rising on my tongue

past life portrait

circa summer 1980

Genius isn't free; there's a great price to pay.
And Richard knew it.
—Jennifer Lee Pryor

When fucking is the family business
you got two choices: hide the bruise

of your shame and cry or look at it
square on and laugh until the bruise

becomes muse or keloided battle scar.
When your daddy is a motherfucker

you learn to remove your pinky ring
before you slap, so not to leave a bruise

or break skin—there is already too much
blood invested in this business when

your granny is selling your mama
and other women's bodies you learn

irony and fucking becomes funny
as fuck except laughter sounds like bruise

and you grow up thinking of women
as sweet things to cop like candy bars.

Pussy is neither exotic nor erotic
but rather ordinary as a bruise

and what's a boy to do but collect
panties and curse words in a house

full of blasphemous Jesuses ricocheting
out of the mouths of tricks—bruised

lips that do not kiss, just suck. What
the fuck you gon' do but laugh?

And make everybody and they mother
laugh too so you don't feel crazy or lonely—

And the laugh tracks start to loop lovely
like the women loop lovely marriage

after marriage every year like some sort
of odd ritualistic undoing of the bruise

of your daddy as pimp and Original
Motherfucker: origin of your laughter

the golden key to your happily ever
after—the records, movies, mountains

of cocaine and fuck and nigger empires
until you understand *nigger* bruises.

When the laughter turns to voices
that won't turn off when the routine ends

and the cocaine only quickens everything
to a blur of fuck, you must confront the bruise

but grandma ain't there to kiss away the hurt
cause she dead along with mama and daddy

so you pick at the scab, grab the rum to silence
the humming in your head with a cigarette lighter.

Poof! You remember running—the skin
tight with scorch   baffling light and bruise

and the clarity is scary as hell
cause you realize the price of genius,

the product of your laughter
and your happily ever after awakens

you in a hospital room that smells
of bandage and damaged blues.

love

big bang theory

for my granny, Lillie Mae Ford

in theory, she big bang.
her brown round lump of a body
stardusting half dozen babies into being
and giving God all the glory.

first Junior, who sprang to 6'4" like his daddy
ate up everything including the cardboard
pickled his tongue in sips of thunderbird
till shriveled liver polka-dotted his hands and lips pink.

Sista came next, wearing Ethel like storm cloud
and hex, shamed her into Angelina, meaning:
messenger of God but she big
and unpretty as a heathen.

Doris Yvonne got *all* the pretty and the skinny
and the crazy, so folks couldn't covet.
at 6, she saw colors fuzzed round people
thought everybody had this rainbow vision.

then in 1952, my mama brown-nosed herself
here. granny named her Amber, a quiet, too-dark
punk of a girl, ass-whippings all the way home
from school. married her fool-self off at 14.

Wayne came out in handcuffs. did not
pass go. went straight to jail. met
Muhammad and became Ramel
became crackhead became ghost.

Pamela named me. cute as she wanna be
spoiled with religion, granny's baby.

spent half her life in the church testifying
to chicken wings, getting her holyghost on.

granny big bang. sequined hat
gangster. kicked Otis senior out
for mucking up her doilies with
engine grease. grandbabies everywhere.

fat as pork rinds and hungry as slaves.
she banged pots til they bled gravy,
banged her big body to the floor
in stroke. invented: *serious as a heart attack.*

she buried all the men with Jesus
on her breath. and when her big-boned
self big-banged to dust, we didn't call
it death. we called it magic.

Sister

for my mother and Auntie Sister

By the time you reach
home, a pack of black mouths
at your back, Sister is leaning
in the doorframe, frowning.

Your pigeon-toed saddle shoes
dust themselves up the driveway.
Your defeated limbs disown you—
wish for a braver body.

At the porch steps, Sister rolls her eyes,
lips pursed. Your sweated-out
bangs, a ghetto visor for your browning
brow. In 1962, the sun still hates niggers.

Sister is lighter, older, heavier, and almost
ugly. This makes her the meanest
person you have ever shared
a bed with, and she can't stand

punks. She palms a broken
broom handle, eyes a piece of chainlink
dangling on the twisted wrought-iron railing,
squints at a rock the size of a shot put,

shakes her head at your helpless self.
And you know that there ain't no coming
home unless you turn 'round, grab the chain,
swing blindly, and fight—the sun, the black

mouths, a chorus of cuss words singing
your praises. Of course, your eyeless
swinging misses, but your fists are sudden
beasts feasting on heat and open mouths.

game recognizes game

In honor of my half-brother Calvin's graduation
from high school, I fool myself down to Virginia
half-curious, full of anger, and burdened by silence.
Solely on the strength of my genetic inheritance,
I am there to show you this mirror: your nose,
eyebrows, turned down mouth, childish pout
to show you how fine I have turned out in spite
of your absence.

When you and Calvin show up, me and Tiffany
are in the garage, knocking balls around
on the pool table. Red-eyed and haggard,
you insult me right off talking bout
what I don't know or something like that.
You say, *I don't get no hug?*
And I say, *no,*
offer you my hand.

Folks have gathered: liquored
and feeling festive. Beer in hand,
I summon my project hustle. Balls scatter,
drop like snitches. All five brothers, tight
with defeat, quietly root for you. I am undaunted
remembering me at ten chopping down dudes
twice my size the cocky rise in my voice yelling,
next!   But you were gone by then.

Your shots are quick and sure, as they should be
in your house, on your table. But when you miss
on the 8, I bank it in the corner, offer my hand
say, *good game.*

hands

i have been preoccupied with my hands. in patches, the dead, yellowed skin on
my palms sheds itself. my hands are not a fan of bleach or dog shit but it takes
one to clean the other. at first, the hands scaled and itched. i scratched so much
in my sleep, my partner, back turned, believed i was masturbating. a filthy floor
requires bleach. even a tomboy knows this by the time she is 7. these hands have
always been wrinkled beyond their age. after years of cracking, the knuckles
on the right require a bigger ring size than the left. my hands are small. too
small for my height. i call them my worker monkey hands—small and good for
fixing shit, for rescuing earrings wedged between car seats. i do not find the
peeling of my hands symbolic. a bit problematic and certainly symptomatic,
but not symbolic. it just is. i joke with my girl that she has put an ugly hand
hex on me to keep me from mojoing any cuties. lesbian hands are important.
at once practical and sexual. they hang blinds and orchestrate orgasms, clean
up dog shit, penetrate asses. they should not be crusty, dry, yellowed, peeling
like mine. a curse, perhaps? no. this is not symbolic. i am at once exasperated
and fascinated by the affliction. i call attention to myself to keep people from
wondering. *look at my hands,* i say, turning my palms toward them. *allergic
reaction, y'know, bleach and shit.* the poets offer remedy: cocoa butter, Shea
butter, coconut oil, olive oil, vitamin E oil, Vaseline. i buy a soap of olive oil and
aloe. the green, chunky square makes my hands stink. i have become obsessed
with the picking. tearing at the skin with my teeth and spitting. prodding the
puckered white spots until the skin unfolds itself. this obsession is not symbolic.
neither are the reddened blotches of tender that are revealed. my fingerprints
are vulnerable swirls of new pink. i rub my hands against my forearms. they
sing a song of sandpaper. i am conscious of hand-shaking, opting to bump fists
instead. this is the second shedding. the first occurred one summer after 9th
grade when i spent every day playing basketball. the rubbery tread of the ball
ripped my hands raw. my hands amuse me. i look at them and can't help but
laugh. on my right thumb, a swatch of skin has puckered in the shape of a heart.
i think of my lady and smile. this is not symbolic.

how to get over
for those of us who can't quite quit her

when the poem flirts
similes hugging her thighs

like a tight skirt: consider
the possibilities.

if the poem follows
you home, whiskey

pickling her tongue:
make her coffee, black.

if the poem arrives
dressed as metaphor,

begging for candy: trick
or retreat till the mask falls.

should the poem slink
outta panties, stand

naked demanding touch:
finger her lines

till her stanzas beg
for an encore: come

again, explore, imagine odd
positions of sweet revision.

and whenever she whispers,
stop: listen and leave her be.

honeysuckle, pussy, and random acts of nature

on summer days when humidity
was full of herself
the sweet smell could smother you

wildly overgrown bushes pushed
into the streets rooted in red clay
their bright white and yellow petals
perfect for small fingers to pluck

pull stamen gently through shaft
until the delicate drop appeared
more a trick of magic than nature
my tongue never knew the difference.

now i know there are acts of nature
i will never comprehend:
how a tree bends in deference

to wind, how ocean can swallow
a city in her dark jaws
spit back lopsided houses,
boardwalks of kindling, dwindling hope.

pussy is an act of nature. i know
having been drenched by her rains,
and honeysuckle is not unlike
pussy. both beckon fingers and suck

both taste of wet grass and dew
watery honey and warm clay
and on a hot summer day

i can smell it for miles and miles.

how to get over

Icarus as woman

gather loose ends, tie in a bundle
kindle with rumor, humor them into a fiery hymn
consider flight, then reconsider on account of a broken wing.
push children from swings, memorize effortless delight
shadowbox colors purpling the horizon foolish
go home smelling of night: all smoke and wonder.

she'll notice singed forearms, inhale twinged wonder
gather question marks thickening the air, a knotted bundle—
toss them to the curb before she calls you foolish
quell her suspicions with song, voice mysterious hymns.
as she sleeps, pleasure yourself into whimpering delight
labia singing the flight of butterfly wings.

morning: things begin to fray, fodder for foolishness
sunlight guilting you for taking her under your wing
every breath an indictment, every sigh a hymn.
skim your memory for yellow, turn bruise to wonder
these things happen, no need to get your heart in a bundle
fight for all that you believe in, delicious necessary delight.

wake her from sleep with sex—sheets a twisted bundle
flex and scatter feather, weather a tumultuous hymn
bed stained blood and splatter, she strokes your wounded wing
you sing pain, strain toward wingspan, a complicated delight
that simpler beings might find foolish.
humble yourself: enjoy unraveling complex wonder.

become thunderbolt. jolt her bones with delight
relish her thighs, lightning quick, threatening your heartbeat foolish
remember loose ends, tie her mouth in a bundle
no word needed now—useless as a broken wing.

refuse the sting of reality puncturing this haze of wonder
reuse every breath—every sigh, every goodbye a recycled hymn.

ignorance is bliss, it's the knowing that's foolish.
she need not know how you prayed yourself to wings
obsessed with flight, freedom became your hymn
sprouting from shoulder blades with reckless wonder
you gathered stray feathers into quiet bundles
winging yourself against blossoming branch, tickled with delight.

but clumsy wing has yet to heal, your nerves all a bundle
wonder what herbs can heal this wounded hymn
no delight in waiting. freefall toward fate: giddy, foolish.

rock. and roll.

when we fuck, clavicles become drumsticks
clanking funk into taut skin tattooed brown
cymbals clash as we thrash breathless quiver
spasmodic legs quick and long as rivers
& as reckless hiss & knock of radiator
multiply heat exponential your sweat:
a necklace of notes beckoning suck. kiss—
till it throbs like blown speakers leaks soprano
hum blurs gospel with flesh bed as mosh pit
we spread-eagle taunt darkness flailing erratic
grit & rhythm act as glue ultramagnetic
holyghost coming orgasmic haint hallelujahing
anointed clitoris cause pussy be a rock star blinded
by spit hoping rhythm'll catch hold of this groan
and thump fucking till eyeliner smears your face
beautiful our breath: a chorus of hymns.

praise song for the sheets

their golden hue   their 300-thread count of semi-softness
bleach stained   sweat stained   spit stained   silent—
they do not complain

of unfamiliar bodies abnormal temperatures
heated arguments after lukewarm
sex

a discarded dildo or vibrating phones tucked
under pillows—they remain
cool.

holding it
together
in spite of

the pistachio shells   spills of whiskey   the fractured breathing
the middle of the night departures when she abandons
us

for the air mattress and there is no one but me   the mosquitoes
and the heat   oh sweet sheets how you remain
cool—

l-o-v-e

even with its selfish, gaping mouth always hungering
for anything that throbs. even with its greedy hands
that rob the day of light. even as it feeds on dust and flux
and flails itself into a dizzying orbit. even if i am but a speck
in its memory—invisible. insignificant. in

destructible.

even if i am fucked from the outset: a willing victim
longing to taste my own bloodsong. even with its inherent
loss and injury—shattered bones, scabs, torn skin. even with
all of its requisite failures. stops and starts. hearts ripped
and thrown to grinder. it is my only reminder that i breathe
and bleed and need. even if this empty hand is my only

success.

blues

she taste like blue all beautifully bruised and melancholy on my tongue like
blue glinting golden   bee-stung and swollen in a field of cotton   like blue
verging black until all memory's forgotten she taste like blues—like Muddy
Waters, like Daughters of the Dust, like Mississippi goddamn   like thrust
and thirst   like heartbreak so new it tastes like trust at first   like a wound
you must nurse with your own salty tears   she taste like blue cause that's
the color of her fears—she taste like blue cause that's the color of her fierce
like an azure hue reminiscent of sky breaking wide open blue like colored
girls who done tried dope when hope wasn't enough—when that man wasn't
enough—when being tough wasn't enough   blue like Nina's voice and storm
clouds   she rains blue-black and sometimes her loyalty is tragic still she blue
like magic   all stardust and confetti and taps of wands and when the house of
cards collapses she come hollering with Jesus on her breath   eyes watery with
devotion   taste like sky and periwinkle and aqua blue like the fifth chakra
vibrating her throat translucent rocking with holyghost trying to shake
loose sin within her blues run deep and honeysuckle sweet like grandmama's
hambone on a Sunday morn blue like early morning beckoning sinners
toward their reckoning blue like night sky sucking up light like a magic trick
tragic as guitar strings breaking like my heart making art outta life all spit-
shined and bruised like the blues of the South a new shade of truth exploding
its name in my mouth. like—

blk

for avery r. young

when i say him the blackest motherfucker i know
what i mean is him done been here

before. this ain't the first sun him skin done seent
him skin a brown bark with all the sad knowledge

of trees. him voice rising sap. even him laughter
branches a blues   him eyes ain't his—maybe

Harriet's so full of trouble and witness him legs
belong to a nigger refugee—three states away

before bullets buckled him legs a reminder
this lifetime and still him acting up   back again

black   bow-legged   pigeon-toed feet full of stomp
and rebel teeth like moonlight a sky full of north

stars lead him to Harold's chicken every chew
church   truth him religion as easy with Jesus

as Southside niggas grandmas youngbloods
whitefolk—him smile disarming him dark skin

spitshine and holyghost, shadowbox and hustle
him voice a field of indigo a blueblack chorus

of alla them 'n' 'em
gone before us

death she deserved

In 1943, Dr. Willem Kolff, a doctor working during the Nazi occu-
pation of the Netherlands, built the first working dialysis machine
using "sausage casings, beverage cans, a washing machine, and
various other items that were available at the time."

the way i remembered it Nana died on a dialysis machine
which saddened me to think (once i had learned what it meant)
this was the death she deserved.

made me think how interchangeable: oxygen, blood, water—
the imagined tubes, water wicked from blood,
a cumbersome & inefficient replacement.

made me think how tubes, gears, pumps cannot be a kidney
nor can sausage casings, juice cans,
a washing machine.

no matter how advanced technology convinces itself
it is still a crude substitute for a lung which made me think
of how my Nana really died—

of emphysema in a bathroom stall at a church revival.
made me think how expendable a lung is:
hubris, a pollutant. how a registered nurse

smoked a pack a day and praised God with those same tainted
lungs   how they found her on her knees perhaps
wheezing a prayer between coughs.

made me think how interchangeable: kidneys, lungs—
memory—   history—   water, blood, oxygen
how turbines, flashing lights, compressed air

cannot replace a lung or two, but Nana never needed
such contraptions having collapsed dizzy from deprivation
realizing how her prayers could not replace breath.

die

stinky nigger bitch with a bush on her head

for the white woman who said it
circa 2012, Oakland

some years ago when this country
was either slaves or masters
some *stinky nigger bitch with a bush on her head*
pushed a titty in your great great grandmama's mouth

got *stank* from master wrestling her to dirt
ripped rags, the unyielding white weight all blur
sweat smeared—fear tinged spit. an armpit
in her face with no choice but to taste that stink

got *nigger* pelted upside her head like rocks
a chorus of hands just a slinging   *nigger*
muddying her blackberry skin with bruise
a four-hundred-year tattoo refusing to fade

got *bitch* cut 'cross her face like a blade
for birthing fair-skinned babies with master's face
bitch dangling scarlet from her dark neck
ain't no dodging this judgment   this taint

got *bush on her head* from her mama
'n' them   African acrobats in shit   only two arms
and a village to carry on they heads—baskets
of yams, gourds of water, firewood

got *bush* from the bush, tangle of hair,
all of Africa in a bundle and everythang
you fear: spears, Voodou, bones, juju
it filled with magic, bitch—make a wish

past life portrait

circa 1849, after Harriet

a bodiless field overgrown with rotting cotton. a silent loom, an empty room invisible indigo stained hands. a hint of a scent: sugar cane aflame. a lopsided framehouse still stands—i, stand still, smile while history gets the lighting right. there i am merely blur and streak   becoming   body-less.   a faint haint ghosting aperture.

a sunset purples like a bruise, a bodiless tree weeps its lassoed branch—stench of lynching. peaches flinch and shrivel. cane gone sour. a rumless punch. a fist and a shotgun conspire against horizon. its flagrant glow. we only know night-fall—face of haze and shadow. a dusty afro of forgotten cotton. a rusty hoe. a hole digging itself.

past life portrait

summer 1919

abhorrence. a/head. abnormal angle. a burnt body beyond barbecue.
charred. chewed disintegration. damage done. dangle. every eye fixed.
fascinated. failed fruit. goodness gracious. goddamn. hounds holla high-
haired. hungry. intuit insurrection. insubordination. intoxicated injustice.
Jesus. jury kills kids looking. licking lips. munching moonpies. mammie's
milk. mmmhhh. mmmmhhh. motherfucking monkey movie. mutilated
niggers only. pack picnics. point 'pon poorboy's penis. quite queer.
resurrection remix. rock racist rhythms. rejoice. reformed rapist swings
solemn. some Sunday. some shine. some sad smile. teeth tell the truth.
under vermillion. white white. yesterday's yell zigzags.

ars poetica

perhaps concrete is a truth
we'd rather not—its teeth
made of dogshit & shell casings

it splits kneecaps & bloodies
itself with brown bodies the mind's
eye does not care to see.

still life—color study

July 13, 2013

Saturday afternoon: in the driveway between buildings they blow up
balloons—yellow, red, blue—for a 3-year-old's party.

The intermittent pops startle me like random gunfire—remind me
of birthdays brown boys will no longer celebrate.

The DJ, having set up the speakers, begins to play—the music, a rapid fire
of bass thump, commandeers the apartment. We have no choice but leave.

An art show: canvases colored with boxes and lines—a grid of red
on a backdrop of yellow. We speak of the abstract with wine in our mouths.

Meanwhile, in an antechamber, six are sequestered. They speak of mali-
cious intent, blood, evidence, testimony—murder versus manslaughter.

We arrive home to a throng of brown bodies, hands clutching red cups,
and music: its insistent treble stabbing the ears.

Inside, we slam all windows, but the music still blares as my niece shoots
people on the video game—its sounds are too realistic to bear.

Instead, the news, a verdict is in: not guilty. And everything is a blur
of sound, my heart beating so fast I put a hand to my chest.

I watch the TV screen: a collage of abstractions—spotlights, microphones,
smiles, handwritten signs. I stare, as if it were a painting—

a smear of twisted faces smothered in gesso and oil, a grid of red
on a backdrop of yellow—to make sense of.

The party continues. The 3-year-old probably in bed dreaming of melted
ice cream, and I am tired of partying.

There is a police station a half block away and I want it to burn. Instead, only the smoke of weed, the meaningless music droning on,

the popping of balloons. Sunday morning, the birds are angry—their chirping a noisy chant: NO NO NO NO. Outside, the rubbery flesh

of balloons color the driveway like splotches of paint. In an instant, those still lives of heave and breath—gone in a pop.

bodega dreams

in the dream the teeth are a Basquiat crown
an upside-down ghost of chalked triangles
whistling rotten   up   there   a spotlight
of glass   an 8mm bodega
in slow motion   surveillance   a crew of
fitted hats   tossing gallons   to the floor
a river of Organic Milk rushing from
the door   the teeth smile at its missing milk
down   there   hipsters clutch cups— lap up this
ghetto harvest   lactose abundance   invisible
negroes   got white folk   intolerance
and the cups ain't got no ears—deaf to the *Jaws*
anthem   the hungry teeth   gnashing
limbs tattooed pale   the bloodied milk

you ain't seen nothing yet

underneath the floor's unforgiving squeak
lives a boy forever
crying

i wonder the shape of his tears: bulbous
diameter of saltwater

how might i measure the radius of his grief?
how many droughts
could

be solved by this
unhappy child?

some days i long to braid his tears
into song—other days
i want

to collect the sour milk breath
of each wail

in a mason jar and carry it off
into the world:
show

this lil boy what sadness
is all about.

brownboy dreams

in the dream a brownboy
is walking a black plastic
bag attached to a piece
of twine across the street
like a puppy dog—

the plastic bag is smiling
its black eyes shining
in the streetlight
its wavering body
a breeze—

the night is unpredictable
as a street fight a beat cop
yelling *freeze!*
his black eyes shining
the gun's wavering body—

a sneeze erupts a gun
goes *pow!* mouths open
like a silent movie a chorus
of wows   black plastic bag
knocked-up by a vodka bottle—

nine minutes later
an alcoholic is born
mouth open like a plastic bag
he look just like his mama
that brownboy did too—

past life portrait

Rodney King on Radio Raheem

fuck getting along that coulda been me
i mean all the man wanted was
a couple of brothas on the wall
extra cheese on his slice
twenty D batteries
Public Enemy on blast
to rep Bed-Stuy to the fullest
and walk thru the hood
without getting wet

how you gon' smash a Black man's radio
and not expect to get choked
money snatched from the register
shit set on fire?

i mean, how you gon' beat a Black man
on video
so's his own mama can't recognize him
and expect niggas not to go apeshit?

they ain't have to kill him though
choke him till his eyes turned phantoms
till he was beatboxing spit
Air Jordans just dangling

everybody was at the funeral
Mookie even wore church shoes
Buggin' Out combed his hair
Smiley wailed till they calmed him outside

in the coffin
Radio Raheem

looked peaceful,
they said
hands 'cross his chest
          love
     hate
glowing golden
'cross his fingers.

trouble man

for Marvin Gaye

honest to god   your voice
had nothing to do with church
hypocrite holler, holy roller shout
down the aisle eyes spirited white—
no. your wail and devilish pelvis
reeked of Saturday night sin

when you sang butterflies
sprang from your mouth
and silenced the land
honeycomb soul dripping
from your lips—you oozed
sex. boozed, coked, choked
brilliance into a dull flicker
mirrors refused to reflect

paranoia filled your head with whispers
voice scraped of its sweet only the raw
remained sandpapered down to spittle
little mason jars lined the window
where daddy collected your dreams
each one perfect—shaped like a bullet

homegoing

for Whitney

what else beyond this light? this flight of color. this
accidental plunge toward blue. this
lunge and tussle. this wilting muscle. this
drunken stutter. this eyeless stare. this circumstance. this
pomp. this stomp and holla and falling to knees.
this final plea. this hollow shell. this
scrutiny and tempt, grunt and snort. this
last resort. this aching voice. this heart racing itself toward stop. this
thump and flop. this broken-winged bird in my lung. this
gasp. this grasp and release. this breath verging cease. this
rasp of voice. these bruised wrists. this fist undone. this
open palm. this sudden calm. this lightness. this
submerge into white. this dead silence. this
light . . .
what lies beyond

                                                     this?

these sinking bones no longer urge toward song. this
surge. this pure purge of breath. this
light—
in Jesus's name. this
warm miracle in my throat
these swallowed flames.

mourning (for fuck's sake)

when you speak i listen
for light to leak from the slit
of your slut-mouth glistening
illustrious strut of breath
chanting tantrum
even the perfume of your spit
dizzies me toward crave

oh how your thighs misbehave
threaten to snap my neck
wishbone-quick suck till you are stuck
in my throat like fishbone swallow
all that is hollow and ache i live
to take what you give and fuck
till you break open all swollen and throb

sobbing songs your mama used
to hum   mourning her gone
and longing to numb   my thumb
a joystick inside you—nightmare
jolts mid-slumber every sleep
a brown-eyed death i say she's there
to guide you but feels more like a haunting

taunting breath's return   the smiling
sight of her uninvited lingers—
these fingers press through void
in search of scripture shredding
your lips like ripped bible pages
this fuck rages strapless
until scraps of brown paper skin

litter this bed of sin and thief
stealing grief with each thrust
till the cops come knocking
and find us dangling musty
every lurking memory
slides white
off our melting teeth.

autopsy of a not dead father

The term "autopsy" derives from the Ancient Greek autopsia, *"to see for oneself"*

My smiling scalpel would be bored
at the sight of your anorexic heart.

There is no medical art in your
corroded lungs or puffs of smoke

escaping distended chest cavity. Your fatty
liver could not seduce this sterile blade.

It would slice through a brigade of veins
defending the still warm blood clotted

under your knotted skin. It would cut
a quick path to bone—home

of memory and the purpose of this inquiry
is to discover what math remains: some distant

number of me that brittled your bones. What
flashbacks have softened the marrow?

A five-year-old me sitting in your lap
behind the wheel of a big, big car. Your

hands atop mine were warm arrows aiming
at some unknown target. What cancer hid

in those bones? Disabled your DNA so you
no longer knew who was of your ribs? Scalpel

demands an answer beyond blood—rough
esophagus with no echo of my name. I must

exist somewhere within your crumbling
vertebrae. Some slipped disc of your paralysis

that kept you from walking back into my life.
What would the chisel reveal scraping the bone

back to cartilage and then to dust? How much
pressure would the mallet require to fracture

humerus? What funny memory stuck
in the splintered shaft would spatter

out a laugh I would not remember?
The organs are useless fodder: my heart

wooden with reckless arrows. Yours
a meal for sparrows in a overgrown

field. The body's beautiful decay yields only
bones. Sun bleached. Scattered without

recall of firstborns wielding scalpels seeking,
for herself, anything that matters.

past life portrait

circa 1989, for Uncle Mel

That night you came knocking—boogeyman haunting
the whites of your eyes,

when you came inside eyes flitting about the room
like a cooped pigeon,

when you unplugged the VCR—wrapped the cord
with a tornado of hands,

when you said *I'm sick, I'm sorry*—we forgave you.
When I opened the door,

let you in, more concerned with some version of perfect—
maybe it was *The Cosby Show,*

or some other Thursday night rerun my eyes refused
to release—I turned my back

and forgave you as I plopped on the couch next to Tiffany
watching as you whipped

the wire into a frenzy—the VCR's black bulk against your chest,
your eyes a blank page

yearning. Our mouths forgave you even if the only word we knew
was: *no.* Our slow-motion

heads blurring the screen blue. We forgave you—your back,
the door slamming us silent.

We watched the rest of the show as if you had been
a commercial. A familiar ghost—

my mother's brother, Irish twin—she eleven months your senior
singing that same ol' song: *I'm sick . . .*

we forgave you: ain't like we had no videotapes anyway
and at least you didn't take the TV.

bop: Miss Cleo can't save you

in 1985, Crack raped my mama
gnawed her blackbottom down to the bone
a skeleton in our closet bathroom   backroom
transistor drone and static we heard when
ears stuck to the door   suctioning sound
deciphering suck from gluttonous moan

where are your hips, mama?
whittled away like a pastime   paradise
lost its swag   swig of backwash from brown
paper bags Crack sucked your titties saggy
tagged frown lines on your forehead like graffiti
choked your voice into reedy whisper sinister
rasp of denial while we witnessed your magic:
making TVs disappear.

vanished your laughter into gasp huff
they fired your ass from the Winn-Dixie
when your till came up short   came home
with a bag full of bruised fruit—locked your door
poplocked and puffed till flame bougalooed blue
rock   rock   planet rock   don't—stop.

how to get over

for Auntie Evon

trip the light ecstatic   x-ray prism vision
black folk cloaked in broken rainbows but what
we know?   glow ultraviolet   grow your own weed
call it *vegetables*   cultivate seeds sliding slick
against a Rick James album cover   rock two Indian
braids & a turban   wear a disturbing amount of purple
lavish lavender upon us earthlings with weak

frequencies following the wrong calendar
suffer Sundays no more—barefoot hallelujah
to the Jefferson's theme song   dream beyond
the halo of Jesus   his miraculous glow
& what aura he rockin?   ain't i your golden child?
Auntie be a Prince song   cuz there is *joy in repetition*
run up the light bill with Lauryn Hill's soulful wail

this life   this young sun your burden to carry
remarry? unlikely   niggas not worthy   instead
bury your heart in a movie screen   done seen
every *Rocky*   know every *Last Dragon* scene
do a mean Shonuff impression: *catching bullets*
wif yo teef?!   *nigga please!*   memorize the kiss
between Taimak & Vanity   their celluloid bliss

you gift me my ego   gift me my gift before
it had a bow or know its presence   gift me
my golden myself at 10 years old   my beloved
le tigre windbreaker   circa 1983   remember
me   uprocking gym floors before class?   you
gift me my badass   my tomboy   my ghetto joy
gift me bourgie & chocolate covered strawberries

and now as i listen to Natalie Merchant's
"kind and generous" as you did over & over
a sudden melancholy becomes me
because i know your tired body was no
longer a vessel of light but of smoke
& Coors light   & i know how your onliest
beat the fight out of you   how Celie's blues

became your bruised scripture   how rage simmered
so long   it volcanoed into rupture
now you elsewhere   all pulse & fluorescent
glow   on the day of your funeral tiffany
sermons forgiveness   & i   8000 miles away
wonder the color of your dress   the rest is easy
Auntie   rest easy, Auntie   *& thank you   thank you*

Notes

"how to get over *Donyale Luna*" is an inspired by the point of view of Donyale Luna, arguably America's first Black supermodel although Donyale wasn't interested in the accolade. Rather, she preferred to point out her Mexican and Irish ancestry. She achieved some level of success, which was short-lived due to an overdose at the age of 33.

"black, brown, and beige (a movement in three parts)" was inspired by a symphony of the same name composed by Duke Ellington. It premiered at Carnegie Hall in 1943 to mixed critical reviews. It was Ellington's ambitious attempt to render the history of the Negro in America via music. The italicized titles in each section correspond with Ellington's original song titles.

"past life portrait *machete, circa 1791*" refers to the beginning of the slave revolt in Saint-Domingue that eventually led to Haiti's independence.

"past life portrait *whip, circa 1793*" recalls the whip's insidious purpose to punish slaves recovered from escape attempts especially after the Fugitive Slave Act of 1793 was passed.

The idea for "past life portrait *circa 1787, Negroes Burying Ground, Lower Manhattan*" comes from Carla L. Peterson's *Black Gotham*. In particular, Chapter One, which details how medical students, also known as "resurrectionists," dug up the bodies of Black people to be used for study.

In "ode to an African urn," the italicized text is taken from Keats's "Ode on a Grecian Urn," specifically the first and fourth stanzas.

"how to get over *for Kardin Ulysse*" was inspired by a news article that reported on June 5, 2012, Kardin Ulysse, a 14-year-old middle-schooler was jumped by four boys in the lunchroom and called a *fucking faggot, transvestite,* and *gay.* Beaten so badly, Kardin can no longer see out of his right eye.

"past life portrait *circa 1940, Lorain, Ohio*" considers the setting of Toni Morrison's first novel, *The Bluest Eye.* It specifically references Pecola, the novel's tragic character who longs for blue eyes.

"wilding" is dedicated to Antron McCray, Kevin Richardson, Raymond Santana, Kharey Wise, and Yusef Salaam, also known as the Central Park Five. In 1990 they were tried and convicted of charges ranging from assault, riot, rape, and attempted murder. Their convictions were vacated after serial rapist Matias Reyes confessed to the attack.

"past life portrait *circa 1948, Peoria, Illinois*" considers Richard Pryor's grandmother, Marie Carter, who ran a brothel where his mother worked. Richard is 8 years old in 1948. Two years later, his mother would abandon him to be raised solely by his grandmother.

"past life portrait *circa summer 1980*" attempts to understand Richard Pryor's headspace after his suicide attempt where he poured rum all over himself and lit himself on fire.

"past life portrait *circa 1849, after Harriet*" is inspired by Harriet Tubman's year of liberation—1849, when she escaped from the Poplar Neck Plantation, thus freeing herself.

"past life portrait *summer 1919*" references the year in American history known as The Red Summer where Black folks in cities across the country clashed with white folks while resisting white supremacy.

"still life—color study *July 13, 2013*" refers to the day the verdict was rendered in the George Zimmerman trial. Zimmerman was found not guilty in the shooting death of Trayvon Martin.

"past life portrait *Rodney King on Radio Raheem*" imagines the real life Rodney King's thoughts about fictional character Radio Raheem. The 1989 film, *Do the Right Thing*, featured the character Radio Raheem (played by Bill Nunn). In the film, Radio Raheem is strangled by a police officer. Three years later, police were acquitted of the brutal videotaped beating of Rodney King that had occurred the year before.

"bop: Miss Cleo can't save you" refers to "Miss Cleo," a 900-number psychic "for entertainment purposes only" who advertised on television during the late '90s. The poem utilizes a form invented by Afaa Michael Weaver during a Cave Canem poetry retreat.

Biographical Note

t'ai freedom ford is a New York City high school English teach-
er and Cave Canem Fellow. She received her MFA in Fiction
from Brooklyn College. Her fiction has appeared in *Black Ivy,*
The Brooklyn Review, Bronx Biannual, and *Kweli.* Her poetry
has appeared in *Drunken Boat, Sinister Wisdom, No, Dear, The*
African American Review, Vinyl, Muzzle, Poetry and others. Her
work has also been featured in several anthologies including
The BreakBeat Poets: New American Poetry in the Age of Hip-
Hop. In 2012 and 2013, she completed two multi-city tours as
a part of a queer women of color literary salon, The Revival.
In 2014, she was the winner of *The Feminist Wire's* inaugural
poetry contest judged by Evie Shockley. She was a 2015 Cen-
ter for Fiction Fellow and The Poetry Project's 2016 Emerge-
Surface-Be Poetry fellow. t'ai lives and loves in Brooklyn, but
hangs out digitally at shesaidword.com